P9-BYR-788

CONTENTS

MODDING
Minecraft®

Sarah Guthals, PhD
Stephen Foster, PhD
Lindsey Handley, PhD

WILEY

MODDING MINECRAFT®

Published by
John Wiley & Sons, Inc.
111 River Street
Hoboken, NJ 07030-5774

www.wiley.com

For general information on our other products and services or to obtain technical support, please contact our Customer Care Department within the U.S. at 800-762-2974, outside the U.S. at 317-572-3993, or fax 317-572-4002.

Wiley also publishes its books in a variety of electronic formats. Some content that appears in print may not be available in electronic books.

Library of Congress Control Number: 2015947351

ISBN 978-1-119-17727-2 (pbk); ISBN 978-1-119-17728-9 (ebk); ISBN 978-1-119-17729-6 (ebk)

This book was produced using the Myriad Pro typeface for the body text and callouts, and Bangers for the chapter titles and subheads.

Manufactured in the United States of America

10 9 8 7 6 5 4 3 2 1

PROJECT 4: CAPTURE THE FLAG 97

INTRODUCTION

SO YOU WANT TO MOD MINECRAFT — THAT'S A GREAT IDEA!
You're about to be transformed from a Minecraft *player* into a
Minecraft *modder*. To get there, you have to code. You can handle
it, because you'll use skills you already have — logic, creativity,
math, gaming, and problem solving — to design, build, test,
and share Minecraft mods. This book tells you everything, from
building a large arena to making a multiplayer game that you
can play *inside* Minecraft with your friends.

ABOUT MINECRAFT AND LEARNTOMOD

Minecraft modding used to be only for expert coders. Not
anymore. LearnToMod helps students just like you through
the challenges of Minecraft modding. It explains coding ideas
and shows how much fun it can be to start making mods.
LearnToMod has over 200 badges that guide you, but you can
make your own mods.

The LearnToMod online software teaches you how to make
modifications, or *mods,* that you can run in the multiplayer
version of Minecraft on your very own Minecraft server.

Get LearnToMod at mod.learntomod.com. With this book,
you get free access to LearnToMod for 60 days. Go to
www.dummies.com/go/moddingminecraft for the trial
information.

ABOUT THIS BOOK

Modding Minecraft has projects that help you design, build, and
test each mod, from start to finish. You can play these minigames
inside Minecraft. The earlier mods are simpler, so you might want
to try the projects in order.

How are you going to see what code to enter if I'm not there with you? I'll show instructions and code examples — actual pictures of my screen.

Code is in monofont. If you're reading this as an ebook, you can tap web addresses to visit websites, like this: www.dummies.com.

Some figures will have a magnifying glass, like you see here. The glass is drawing attention to the parts of the screen that you use. The highlighted text draws your attention to the figure.

Working with LearnToMod is super simple: I just give you steps like "Drag a function into the programming environment" or "Click the Minecraft category and then Players." Or I may tell you to click a link or a tab.

ABOUT YOU

Everybody has to start somewhere, right? I had to start writing this book by assuming that you're comfortable doing this stuff:

- » **Typing on a computer and using a mouse.** You may know how to use a Windows system or a Mac; either one will do. All coding takes place in a web browser — and on any browser on either platform. This book shows LearnToMod on a Mac using the Chrome browser.

- » **Getting around on a website.** You can click a link or find a website easy peasy.

» **Playing Minecraft.** You don't need to be a Minecraft expert and you don't have to know how to code. You can play on Windows or a Macintosh, but you have to use the desktop version. The Pocket Edition, which is played on mobile devices, doesn't work with LearnToMod.

» **Doing basic math.** That includes adding whole numbers (like 2+2), and logical operations (like knowing that 3 is more than 2).

ABOUT THE ICONS

As you read through the projects in this book, you'll see a few icons. The icons point out different things:

Watch out! This icon comes with important information that may save you from trouble that modders sometimes have.

The Remember icon comes with ideas that you should keep in mind.

The Tip icon marks advice and shortcuts that can make modding easier.

The Fun with Code icon describes how the modding you're doing relates to the bigger picture of coding.

PROJECT **1** START MODDING

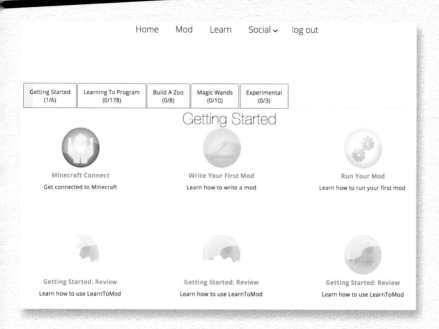

Home   Mod   Learn   Social ⌄   log out

| Getting Started (1/6) | Learning To Program (0/178) | Build A Zoo (0/8) | Magic Wands (0/10) | Experimental (0/3) |

Getting Started

Minecraft Connect
Get connected to Minecraft

Write Your First Mod
Learn how to write a mod

Run Your Mod
Learn how to run your first mod

Getting Started: Review
Learn how to use LearnToMod

Getting Started: Review
Learn how to use LearnToMod

Getting Started: Review
Learn how to use LearnToMod

IN THIS PROJECT, I EXPLAIN HOW TO USE THE LEARNTOMOD ONLINE SOFTWARE. I also explain how to connect to the LearnToMod multiplayer Minecraft Server, and show you how to use the basic tools, such as invisible robots, that you need in order to make your own, fun-filled mods.

KNOW WHAT MINECRAFT MODDING IS

Video games are made up of code. Thousands of lines of code. Code that lets players — players like you — explore new worlds and interact with characters.

Some games, like Minecraft, let players add their own code to create new worlds, challenges, or characters.

Mods, *which is short for modifications (or changes), can be almost any task. A task is something you do, like create a tower or make a mountain explode with TNT.*

You can make these tasks by using mods:

» **Texture:** Change the way the world looks by loading a new texture pack.

» **Block interaction:** Cause an explosion whenever the player destroys a `wood` block type.

» **New block:** Create new blocks, like an `ultra-TNT` block that makes a bigger explosion.

» **Minigame:** Create a minigame within a world. The projects in this book help you do that.

» **Large structure:** Create huge structures (that would take a long time to make by hand but take no time with code).

USE THE LEARNTOMOD ONLINE SOFTWARE

The LearnToMod online software walks you through coding challenges. When you complete a challenge, you earn a badge. Check out the next sections to get started with LearnToMod.

Get the LearnToMod online software at mod.learntomod.com.

This is the software that you'll use for the projects in this book. The badges will lead you through learning coding and different ways to make neat mods.

SIGN UP FOR LEARNTOMOD

It takes about five minutes to sign up for LearnToMod. To sign up for the software, follow these steps:

1 **In a web browser, go to mod.learntomod.com.**

2 **Fill out the Sign Up form.**

   Another dialog box opens.

3 **In the top of the dialog box, type the access key that you got in this book.**

4 **Make a nickname.**

5 **The *dashboard* (also known as the *home screen*) opens.**

|Here's my clever nickname

People will see your nickname anytime you share your mods, so don't use your real name.

USE THE LEARNTOMOD BADGES

To access the LearnToMod coding challenges, follow these steps:

1 **Go to mod.learntomod.com.**

2 **Fill in the Log In form. Use the email address and password you signed up with.**

The home screen opens.

3 **To see the list of challenges, click the Learn tab.**

The first set of coding challenges appears.

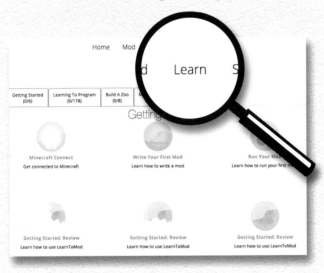

When you finish a challenge, its badge gets colored. You haven't earned badges that are pale, like the ones you see when you click the Learn tab for the first time.

CONNECT YOUR MODS TO MINECRAFT

Just click the first badge: Minecraft Connect. This badge tells LearnToMod what your Minecraft account is. That way, when you open up Minecraft and connect to the LearnToMod server, your mods will be there waiting for you. I explain more about that later.

In this badge, you can find all the instructions to help you connect your mods to Minecraft so that you can see their effects in the game. In this section, I summarize those steps for you.

To run your mods in Minecraft, make sure you have the most recent version of Minecraft.

To see which version of Minecraft you're running, follow these steps:

1 **Click the Edit Profile button in the lower-left corner of the Minecraft startup screen.**

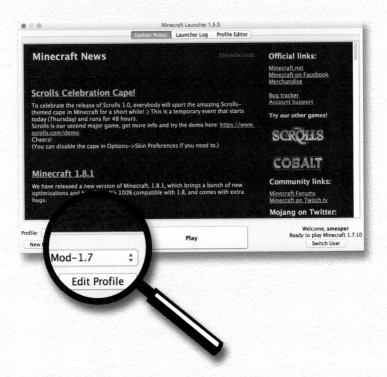

The Profile Edit dialog box opens.

2 **In the Profile Name text box, type the new profile.**

Your profile name can be anything — like ModWorld, for example.

3 **Look at the Version Selection part. In there, the Use Version text box tells you which version you're using.**

You should be using the version at the top of the list. In this case, it's version 1.8. By the time you read this, it might be version 8.1. They're always updating.

4 **If you're using the wrong version, click the up arrow all the way to the right of the Use Version text box. Change it to the most recent version.**

5 Click the Save Profile button at the bottom of the screen.

6 Back in the Minecraft Connect badge on LearnToMod, type your Minecraft username.

7 Type your username in the text box on the badge.

Enter the minecraft username below, and press connect.

YourMinecraftUsername   Connect

Your Minecraft username is added to the LearnToMod account.

Your username must be spelled — and capitalized — exactly the same as you created it. If it isn't, you can't see your mods. When capitalization matters, it's called case sensitive.

8 Click the Connect button.

The Minecraft Connect badge pops up.

Under the text box in the Minecraft Connect badge, you see "Success."

CONNECT TO THE LEARNTOMOD SERVER

With LearnToMod, you can play in either Creative mode or Survival mode, whichever you prefer.

Follow the steps that you see onscreen in the Minecraft Connect badge:

1 Click **Play on the Minecraft home screen.**

2 Choose **Multiplayer.**

3 Click **Add Server.**

4 Type Learn To Mod **as the server name.**

5 Type play.learntomod.com **as the server address.**

6 Click **Done.**

7 Click **Join Server.**

This world is what you should see. It's like a waiting room. You can explore this world while Minecraft finds a new world (where you can test your mods). You probably won't have to wait more than 5 minutes. Be patient — it's not too long!

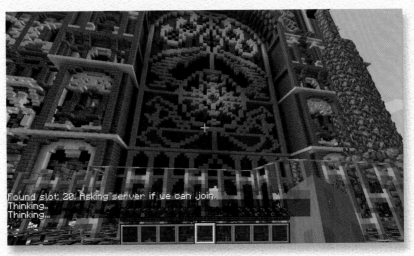

When you're connected to your testing world, there's a mod chest in your inventory.

If you can't connect to the LearnToMod server, email the technical support team at learntomod@thoughtstem.com and explain the trouble you're having.

CHECK OUT THE CODING ENVIRONMENT

Before you begin your modding adventure, check out the coding environment you'll use. Just follow these steps:

1 **Click the Learn tab at the top of the LearnToMod website.**

You're taken to the first set of coding challenges.

2 **Click the Write Your First Mod badge.**

You see the coding challenge.

Take a look at these areas of the page:

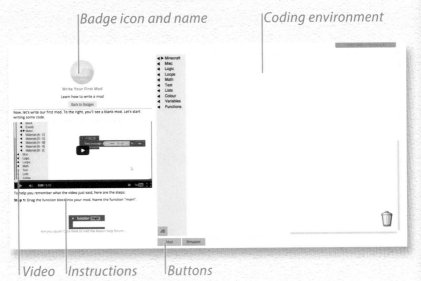

Badge icon and name   Coding environment

Video   Instructions   Buttons

» The upper left shows the badge name; its large, round icon; and the Back to Badges button.

You can click the Learn tab at the top of the screen to return to the list of badges.

» The bottom left has instructions. A short video is always there to explain the coding challenge, and it's followed by a list of steps that tell you what to do.

» The right side shows the coding environment. In this book, you can read how to code using a block-based language that's visual, but you can also try a text-based language.

To get to the block-based code, click one of the code categories (such as Minecraft). Then click and drag a block into the blank coding area. I explain this in the next section.

» The bottom center has two buttons: Mod and Simulator.

» The Mod button sends your mod to the Minecraft testing world.

» The Simulator button opens a Minecraft simulated world in your browser.

TEST YOUR MOD

You haven't finished your challenge yet. You do that in the next section. Use the Minecraft simulator to test your mod and earn the badge:

1 Click the Learn tab at the top of the LearnToMod website.

2 Click anywhere in the simulator area.

3 Complete your challenge.

If you don't get through it, ask for help on the forums by going to forum.learntomod.com, or go to the next badge.

If you get through the challenge, a badge pops up. You can exit by clicking the Back to Badges button and then go on to more challenges.

Badge unlocked!

Write Your First Mod
Learn how to write a mod
Back to Badges

To close the simulator, click the Simulator button again (or press the Esc key on the keyboard).

WRITE A MINECRAFT MOD

When you're ready to write your first Minecraft mod, follow the steps here.

In this section, I help you earn the second badge, Write Your First Mod. You can find these steps in the left column of the badge. Just watch the video or read the instructions.

Make sure you're logged in at mod.learntomod.com before starting with these steps:

1 **Click the Learn tab.**

2 **Click the Write Your First Mod badge.**

3 **Click and watch the video.**

It's on the bottom left of the screen.

To earn the second badge, follow these steps:

1 **Drag a function into the coding environment.**

2 Click the text do something.

3 Type main **to create a** main
function.

4 Click the Minecraft category
and then click Players.

5 Click the Send message **block and drag it to the main**
function.

6 Click the Text category.

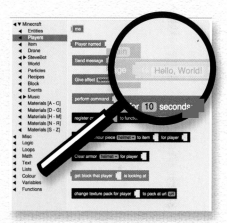

7 Drag the text **block to**
connect it to the Send
message **block. Type**
Hello, World! **inside the**
text **block.**

8 Click the Minecraft
category and then click
Players.

9 Drag the me **block to the second**
space on the Send message **block.**

10 Click the Test in Simulator button (at the bottom of the steps).

11 Click in the simulator. Then press the M key on your keyboard.

You see the message "Hello, World!"

If the simulator (or anything else) doesn't work right, go to forum.learntomod.com and see if anyone has found a solution to your same problem. Or, you can write a post that tells the LearnToMod developers that you found a bug. They'll help you fix it!

12 When the badge pops up, click Back to Badges.

Congratulations! You wrote your first Minecraft mod. In the next section, you test your mod in Minecraft.

Click for Hints (a link at the top right of the screen) can help you. Or ask a question by clicking the Questions or Feedback? link.

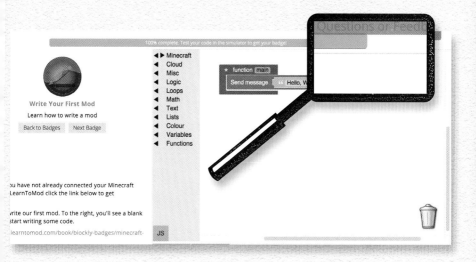

100% complete. Test your code in the simulator to get your badge!

Write Your First Mod

Learn how to write a mod

Back to Badges   Next Badge

- ◀ ▶ Minecraft
- ◀ Cloud
- ◀ Misc
- ◀ Logic
- ◀ Loops
- ◀ Math
- ◀ Text
- ◀ Lists
- ◀ Colour
- ◀ Variables
- ◀ Functions

★ function main
Send message   " Hello, W

ou have not already connected your Minecraft
LearnToMod click the link below to get

vrite our first mod. To the right, you'll see a blank
start writing some code.

learntomod.com/book/blockly-badges/minecraft-   JS

RUN YOUR MOD IN MINECRAFT

After you write your first mod, it's time to run the mod in Minecraft.

If you aren't already in this world, go back to the Minecraft Connect badge and reconnect. Those steps are in the "Connect Your Mods to Minecraft" section.

The third badge, Run Your Mod, spells out the steps and they're given here, too:

1 **Click the Run Your Mod badge under the Learn tab.**

2 **Click the Mod button.**

A message lets you know that the mod was sent to your Minecraft account.

 3 **Click the Minecraft icon. It's on your computer's taskbar.**

You're still in the testing world, so your mod chest is in the inventory.

Now you're going to put stuff in your mod and use it.

4 **Press the 9 key and then click the mouse button.**

The mod chest opens.

5 **Drag to your HotBar the mod that you want to run.**

The HotBar is at the bottom of your inventory.

Hover your mouse over a mod to see its name.

6 **Press the Esc key.**

You go back to playing.

7 **Press the number that goes with the position of the mod in the inventory. Then click the mouse.**

For example, if you place the mod block all the way to the left, press the 1 key and then click the mouse. Now your mod is running.

If you go back to the LearnToMod website at mod.learntomod.com, you'll see that you earned the third badge.

8 **Complete the next three coding challenges, which are quiz questions.**

I won't walk you through those. You're ready to tackle them on your own!

GET READY TO WRITE YOUR OWN MINECRAFT MODS

After you earn at least ten badges, you'll probably get an idea for your own mod. When you're ready to write it, follow these steps:

1 **Go to mod.learntomod.com and click the Mod tab at the top of the LearnToMod online software.**

A new page opens.

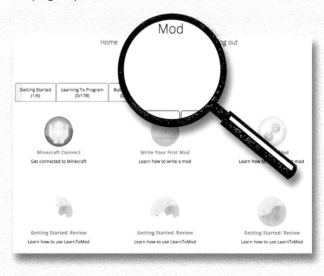

2 Type a title for your mod.

It's best to name your mods something meaningful. For example, if your mod is going to cause Ender Dragons to fill the sky, you might call it Ender_Dragon_Attack.

In coding, spaces sometimes confuse computers — but spaces help people read. Instead of spaces, coders/modders use _ in their names. For example, ender_dragon_attack is much easier to read than enderdragonattack!

3 Click the Blockly (Multiplayer) button.

That creates a *server-side*, or *multiplayer*, mod. A new mod block appears.

4 Click the new mod block to see the mod's description page.

5 Click the Code button.

You see the coding environment.

6 Now you can write a mod.

For example, you could write one that says "Hi" to you. Mine says, "Hi Sarah!"

SHARE A MOD WITH FRIENDS

Writing and testing mods is fun, but having your friends test them in their Minecraft worlds helps you both come up with even more creative ideas.

Sharing a mod with fellow LearnToMod modders is easy. Just follow these steps:

1 Click the Back button in your mod.

2 Click the image box on the top left.

If you haven't already added an image, the box will be a solid color and say Edit This when you hover over it with your mouse.

3 Add a picture and description for the mod.

Just follow the steps on the screen.

4 Click the button to make the mod public.

5 Click the Save button.

It's smart to share mods with friends and ask them to test for you. It's a good way to find bugs and become a better modder.

HOW YOUR FRIEND FINDS YOUR MOD

From here, your friend might need help from you.

1 On her own computer, your friend goes to mod.learntomod.com and logs in with her LearnToMod email and password.

2 Your friend clicks the Find a Mod button.

3 Your friend types your mod name in the Public Mods text box.

Your mod appears. In this example, the mod is named Say_Hello.

4 Your friend clicks and tests your mod.

Your friend also can see your code. Hopefully you'll get some good feedback: What works? What doesn't work? What's really fun or really boring?

If your friend doesn't have a LearnToMod account, you can copy and send the *URL* (the web address) to him. Then he can see your mod, but he can't edit or test it.

BUGS BESIDES BEETLES

Bugs (mistakes in your code) are a part of coding. Because you're human, you will make mistakes — and that's okay! No coder, not even the best ones, writes code perfectly the first time. Code always has bugs in it. To become a better coder/modder, you have to test your code. And ask your friends to test your code, so that you can find the bugs and get rid of them as soon as possible!

EARN MODDING BADGES

You can earn more than 200 badges on LearnToMod! Each badge teaches you a different Minecraft modding trick or coding concept. Scramble and Missing badges are covered here.

You should definitely earn the first six badges under the Learn tab.

EARN SCRAMBLE BADGES

Scramble challenges have all the code blocks you need, and they're already in the programming area — they're just scrambled around on the screen.

To earn a Scramble badge, follow these steps:

1 Test.

Test the right version of the code in the simulator or in Minecraft to see what it's supposed to do.

2 Gather.

Put together all the blocks that have been scrambled on the screen. Just drag them near each other.

3 Unscramble.

Unscramble the blocks and test your mod to see whether it matches the version that you test in Step 1.

To find all the blocks you need for the badge (sometimes, the blocks that have been scrambled are offscreen), move around by using the scroll bars on the right side and bottom.

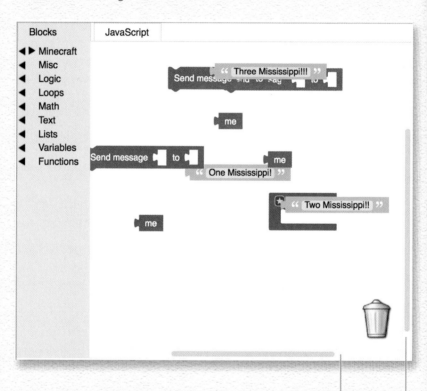

Scroll bars

EARN THE SAYING HELLO BADGE: SCRAMBLE EDITION

You can find the Saying Hello (Scramble) challenge under the Learn tab in the Learning To Program category, and then under Functions. You see ten blocks scrambled on the screen.

Saying Hello (Scramble)

Learn how to create a program that talks to you.

Follow these steps to solve the challenge and earn the badge:

1 **Click the orange test button to test the correct version in Minecraft, or click the blue test button to test the correct version in the simulator.**

Watch what happens.

Computer science is about writing your **own** code. Not just copying code from tutorials (though that's a great way to learn). This puzzle game will help build code writing skills.

Step 0: Press this button to load a mystery mod into your mod chest.

    Add 'saying_hello_variation_1' to mod chest

Or...

    Run 'saying_hello_variation_1' in simulator

2 **Gather the blocks and move them around so that when you run the mod, it does exactly the same thing that the correct version did.**

3 **Test your mod to see whether it has the same effect as the correct version.**

If it doesn't, move the blocks a different way and test again.

4 **Keep moving and testing until it works.**

COMMUNICATE WITH YOUR COMPUTER

Writing code is the way that programmers communicate with their computers, and the way that you communicate with Minecraft. The problem is that computers do exactly what you tell them to do, not what you think they should do. For example, in the Saying Hello (Scramble) challenge, the answer looks strange if you expected the messages to be sent in numbered order, like this:

» One Mississippi

» Two Mississippi

» Three Mississippi

and instead they're sent out of order, like this:

» Two Mississippi

» One Mississippi

» Three Mississippi

If someone said, "Go to your shoes and put on your room," you'd probably figure out that what you should do is go to your room and put on your shoes. If you told a computer, "Go to your shoes and put on your room," the computer would literally go to its shoes and then try to put on its room — which is impossible. It would give you an error message.

You must be precise when you write code, and — more importantly — you should test your code often and just a few lines at a time to catch mistakes.

Two videos are at the bottom of Scramble challenges. Watch them for help getting this type of badge. Even though the videos aren't specific to each challenge, they can help with any badge that asks you to unscramble code.

Here's a video that will teach you a helpful strategy for these kinds of puzzles:

Here's a video that will show you a terrible strategy:

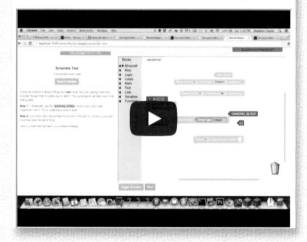

EARN MISSING BADGES

A Missing badge has code that's almost finished. It's just missing a few blocks. Your challenge? Figure out which blocks are missing and where they go. Without those missing blocks, the mod can't run.

As with a Scramble badge, you use a smart strategy to earn a Missing badge. Follow these steps:

1 Identify.

Figure out how many blocks are missing, and see where you need them. Start thinking about what type of blocks might be missing, such as a text block.

2 Test.

Test the correct version of the code in the simulator (by clicking the blue test button) or Minecraft (by clicking the orange test button) to see what it's supposed to do.

3 Follow along.

Follow the code as it's running, and figure out where the missing blocks should go.

4 Add blocks.

Add the blocks and test your code. Does it do the same thing that the correct version does in Step 1? This is what professional coders do: They follow their code while they're testing it, to make sure that they've told the computer to do the right thing.

TRACE CODE

Coders make mistakes, and communicating with computers can be tricky.

Coders (that's you) should be sure to follow the code, before and while it's running, to make sure that they put the lines of code in the right order.

Tracing code is an important skill to master, and you can do it different ways.

» Use the computer. Especially for Missing badges, this is a great way to trace code. First, run the correct code and watch what happens. Then run the code again, but this time point to each line of code as it's being run.

» Use pencil and paper. If you've got a written mod that isn't working the way you expect, draw on paper what's happening after each line of code executes. For example, Send message "Hello, World!" to me will be on the screen, so you should write it down on paper.

EARN THE SAYING HELLO BADGE: MISSING EDITION

Open the Saying Hello (Missing) challenge by clicking the badge. When you earn the badge, the code puts on the screen some lyrics to a Cat Stevens song.

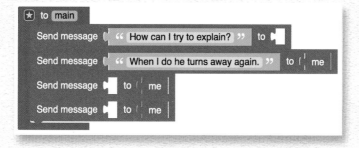

Three blocks are missing from this mod. The first is probably a player block because that's the only player you've used (and that's what the other ones are using). The last two are likely to be text blocks because that's the only kind of message you have sent (and the first two are sending text messages too). It's impossible to guess what text should be in the text blocks, because the list of possibilities is very, very large.

To complete a missing badge, follow these steps:

1 **Run the correct version in Minecraft or the simulator and watch what happens.**

When you run your code, you should see this scene.

The first line of code sends the message How can I try to explain? but doesn't say which player is the message *target* (the one that will get the message). After running the code, the target should be the me block because you can see that message when *you* run the correct version.

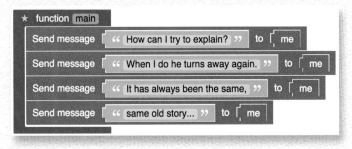

The last two messages are

```
It has always been the same,
same old story . . .
```

Everything sent to me shows on the screen of the person who ran the mod. If you run the mod and you see the message, the target of the message was me.

2 Add the me block and the two text blocks with the correct messages in them.

3 Test your mod.

If you return to a Missing badge or Scramble badge after finishing it, the LearnToMod software asks whether you want to reset the code so that it's missing or scrambled again. If you choose to reset your badge, you'll still have the badge. You just get to do the challenge again.

Some of the projects in this book might be challenging or confusing. If you get stuck, it's always a good idea to earn more badges — they're made to help you understand coding.

PROJECT 2 SPLEEF

Commands Run
smesper

ONE OF THE HARDEST (BUT ALSO FUN!) MINECRAFT MODS THAT YOU CAN MAKE IS A MINIGAME. A *minigame* is a game inside Minecraft.

Spleef is where a player walks around a platform and makes a block disappear by stepping on it. Using just this idea, you can make a lot of different versions of Spleef, like these:

» Players have to try to not fall into the lava that you put underneath the platform. (It's like the version of Lava you play in your living room!)

» After you put lava underneath the platform, and you put other entities (like creepers) in the arena, players try to make the other entities fall into the lava.

» Add platforms on top of each other. Players have to collect items on each level before they fall through to the level beneath.

» In a multiplayer game, players have to try not to fall before the other player falls.

This project shows you how to make a simple Spleef game, and helps you change Spleef to make it your own.

INTRODUCE THE GAMEPLAY LOOP

The gameplay loop is a way to help you figure out your design.

You should always design your code before writing it. It will keep you from getting lots of errors when you code it.

The gameplay loop has four parts:

» **Start:** Create a basic *scene* (the place where your game takes place).

» **Goal:** Add a way to win and lose.

» **Challenge:** Make winning difficult.

» **Reward:** Make players want to win.

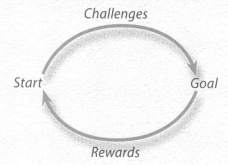

START: CREATE A BASIC SCENE

Start by drawing an idea on paper or building it in Minecraft without mods. Start thinking about how the scene will affect your players. Later, when you build, you can make the arena bigger or add details like colors.

For example, a game where you use the normal Minecraft world is different from a game where you're in a 20 × 20 arena with walls. In the Minecraft world you have never-ending space, but in the arena you only have a 20 × 20 area. You play differently depending on what kind of space you're in.

The design process is iterative, which means that you repeat each step multiple times. That's what the gameplay loop is for. Even if you make a decision early on, you can make a change later.

As you build Spleef, you might start by creating a small world. As you iterate through the gameplay loop (challenges, goals, rewards), you make the world larger — eventually making it infinitely large, as it is today.

GOAL: ADD A WAY TO WIN AND LOSE

Some games may be difficult to make at first.

Just break up the parts of the game according to the gameplay loop pieces. Then you can see a way to make a simple version of the game by creating a basic scene and a way to win (or lose).

For example, if you were playing a super-simple version of Minecraft in Survival mode, the goal would be to not die at night. It wouldn't be hard to survive, because there would be no enemies. That's when you add the simplest feature: the hearts. And you add logic to the game to ask players whether they want to respawn whenever they run out of hearts. Again, at this point the game might not be much fun, but when you reach the next steps (the challenge, followed by the reward), you start to add enemies and ways that players can earn back hearts.

CHALLENGE: MAKE IT HARDER TO WIN

Your game gets interesting when you start making it hard to beat. At first, you might want to offer a small challenge. Don't worry: You can iterate up to the more difficult challenges as you go through the gameplay loop.

For example, in a simple game, the first challenge could be one creeper that tries to attack. This challenge makes the game more difficult. As you iterate through the gameplay loop, you can start adding more creepers or even creatures, and then add items for the player to use as defense.

REWARD: MAKE PLAYERS WANT TO WIN

Who doesn't like to get rewards? A sticker, some candy, a No Homework pass?

Rewarding your players makes your game fun for them. If they're not going to get rewards, what's the point of playing?

Lots of things can be rewards:

» Moving to the next level.

» Items like stars and coins.

» Coins for buying items that help them beat other levels.

In a simple game, you can give a player full health after finding an Instant Health potion. Along the same lines, if the player is playing at the Peaceful difficulty level, just staying alive and not getting hurt is rewarded with health.

PLAN AND TRY TEST CASES

Before playing your mod, figure out the different test cases to make sure that your game is working properly.

Test cases *are different ways to check your mod to make sure it's working.*

Before you write a test case, make two lists that say

» **What you'll test:** For example, breaking the `melon` block.

» **What you think will happen:** For example, the game mode switches to Survival, and blocks below you disappear after one second.

If your test case passes, you know that the mod is correct. If something doesn't do what you thought it should, debug your code.

In Minecraft, you can't tell the game that you no longer want to trigger events.

To trigger an event *means that Minecraft recognizes that the event has happened and then calls the function that was set up in the event call.*

For example, the `SetupPlayer` function has an `event setup` block in it. When the player respawns, this event is triggered after two seconds, and then it sends the player to the middle of the arena.

But you don't always want events to be triggered when you're testing. For example, in Spleef you replace only the block below you with air if you're walking on the arena's `diamond` blocks. If you're playing the Spleef mod and then decide to explore a cave, you start to fall through the ground.

You can get an event to stop triggering. You have two ways to do that:

» Disconnect from the server and reconnect.

 » Open your mod chest. Click the End Events icon.

DEBUG YOUR CODE

Debugging is another step in coding. Not even the best coders write something perfectly the first time. And when a coder — even an expert — makes a mistake, she debugs to find the mistake and fix it.

To *debug* means to go through code, block by block, and make sure it's working. You might have to disable some blocks to run the mod. (Do that by clicking the block and then clicking Disable Block.)

 One of the best ways to debug is to disable all the code expect for a small part, then run the mod to see if it does what it should. (Test it!) If it does work, enable one more line of code and test it again. Keep doing this until you find the one line (or block) of code that gives you the error.

You're going to run into different errors, so I can't fix the problems for you. I can tell you that when you find the block, you'll probably be able to figure out what's wrong by reading your code and comparing what's actually happening to what you *want to have happen.*

MAKE SPLEEF: ITERATION 1

After you know how to use the gameplay loop, you can design and build a single-player minigame.

First, make a new mod by following these steps:

1 **Go to your home page and click Mod at the top of the page.**

2 **Name the mod** Spleef.

3 **Click the Blockly (Multiplayer) button.**

4 **Click the mod tile that gets created.**

My mod tile says See Inside: Spleef by sarah. When you click the tile, the mod page opens.

5 **Click the Code button.**

Now you're ready to make the Spleef game. The rest of the sections help you follow the gameplay loop.

EXPLORE THE ARENABUILDER LIBRARY

The scene on the next page is an arena with a fence around it. To make this arena, you'll use the ArenaBuilder library on LearnToMod.

A library is a mod that's written for you. You can use it without knowing know how it's written.

You should tiptoe through the library to better understand how to build an arena, in case you ever wanted to build your own arena someday. If you want, you can skip to the next section.

To explore the library, follow these steps:

1 **Go to**
mod.learntomod.com/programs/sarah-ArenaBuilder.

You see these five functions:

» `init`

» `move_drone`

» `ArenaWithFence`

» `Platform`

» `Fence`

2 **Click the question mark (?) on a function.**

A comment pops up to describe the function.

3 **Look through the code and see what it's doing.**

Notice a couple things:

» There's no `main` function, because this mod can't run on its own in Minecraft. Mods that don't have a `main` function have to be called from other mods. I explain in the next section.

For a mod to run on its own, a `main` function has to tell Minecraft where to start. If you don't have a `main` function, then Minecraft won't know where to start and won't work.

» The `export` block lets other mods use the function. Other mods can call the functions even though they're in a different mod. Three functions are being exported: `ArenaWithFence`, `init`, and `move_drone`.

4 **Now you can use the `ArenaWithFence`, `init`, and `move_drone` functions in your Spleef game mod.**

START: IMPORT THE ARENABUILDER LIBRARY

After you look through the ArenaBuilder library, go back to your Spleef mod and import that library by following these steps:

1 **Under the Misc category, find the `import` block and drag it into the mod.**

2 **Type** sarah-ArenaBuilder **to replace the text** `lib_name`.

import   sarah-ArenaBuilder

If you enter the name correctly, the block stays green and new functions show up under the Functions category.

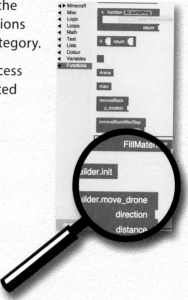

The three functions you have access to are the three that were exported from the ArenaBuilder library: `ArenaWithFence`, `init`, and `move_drone`.

3 Create a `main` function.

To do this, click the Functions category and drag a function block from the sidebar into the programming area. Then click where it says do something, delete that, and type in **main**.

4 Add a call to the `init` function from the ArenaBuilder library.

To do this, click the Function category and drag the `sarah-ArenaBuilder.init` function into the `main` function that you created in Step 3.

Now Minecraft knows where to start reading the code.

This code shows you how to set up your ArenaBuilder.

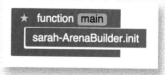

5 Add a call to the `ArenaWithFence` function from the ArenaBuilder library to the `main` function.

To do this, click the Functions category and drag the `sarah-ArenaBuilder.ArenaWithFence` function into your `main` function.

6 **Fill in the five spaces where you can connect other blocks to this function.**

They're called *parameters*.

» Set FenceHeight to 5. Numbers are under the Math category.

» Set PlatformSize to 20.

» Set PlatformWidth to 1.

» Set ArenaMaterial to type DIAMOND_BLOCK. To get to it, click the Minecraft category and then click Materials [D-G].

» Set FillMaterial to AIR. To get to it, click the Minecraft category and then click Materials [A-F] category.

This code makes a 20 × 20 arena made of diamond with a fence that's five blocks high and a platform width of one block. The arena will be filled with air. This makes the arena where you'll play Spleef.

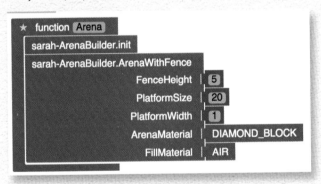

7 **Make sure that the mod is saved, click the Mod button, and test the code in Minecraft.**

You see your scene.

Because you're an ace at following instructions, you already finished the LearnToMod Run Your Mod badge to learn how to test your code inside of Minecraft.

8 Refactor the code:

» Create a new function (the same way you created your `main` function) and call it `Arena`.

» Move the call to `sarah-ArenaBuilder.init` and `sarah-ArenaBulding.ArenaWithFence` into the `Arena` function.

» Go to the Functions category and drag the call to the `Arena` function into your `main` function.

In this case, you're refactoring the code so that the arena is built in a function named `Arena` and so that the arena function is called from `main`.

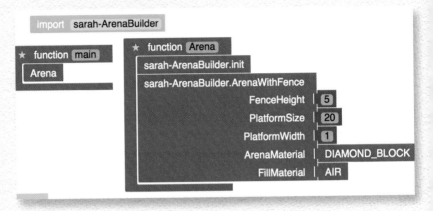

Congratulations: You created the basic Spleef scene! That's a nice reward, huh?

Refactor means to change it without changing what it does.

GOAL: MAKE A WAY TO WIN AND LOSE

When you have an arena, it's time to make a way for the player to win and lose. The easiest versions of the goal for Spleef are these:

» **Win:** You win if you stay on the diamond platform.

» **Lose:** You lose if you fall through the platform.

It's impossible to lose right now because players don't make the blocks below them disappear. However, you can still make the players fall through the platform.

First, make sure that players start in the right place and know what to do when they respawn. The steps in this section help you do this. (The next section adds a challenge: Blocks disappear one second after being touched.)

To set up the winning and losing conditions for Iteration 1 of Spleef, follow these steps:

1 **Add a call to the ArenaBuilder's `SetArenaCenter` function at the end of the `Arena` function.**

The `SetArenaCenter` function is in the Functions category because you imported my ArenaBuilder mod, and I exported the `SetArenaCenter` function.

This step finds the middle of the arena so that the player can be moved there for the start. You can see the added call to `SetArenaCenter` in the `Arena` function.

`SetArenaCenter` also creates a `melon` block, which can start the game. The `melon` block is on the platform. Make sure you see it before moving on.

VARIABLES VARY

A *variable* is a way to name information or data. It's sort of like this: My name is Sarah and I know that when people say "Sarah," they're talking to me. A variable is a way to name data so that the computer knows how to talk to it or use it. Some variables are simple. Some variables are more complicated.

Variables have a box with two sections: NAME and DATA.	**\<NAME\>** **\<DATA\>**
This variable is named num and has the data 5. Simple.	**num** **5**
This variable is named name with the data Sarah. Simple.	**name** **Sarah**
This variable shows the info parameter for an event function associated with a block (that is, the block_break event). info has a block for its data. The block has a type for its data, and the type's data is Melon Block. Complicated!	**info** **block** type Melon Block

2 **Make a new function named** `StartGame` **that takes info as a parameter.**

The game starts when the player breaks the `melon` block.

```
★ function StartGame with: info
    set block ▼ to [ info ▼ 's block ]
    set block_type ▼ to [ block ▼ 's type ]
    ★ if [ block_type ▼ ] =▼ [ MELON_BLOCK ]
    do   perform command  " gamemode s "  for player [ me ]
```

3 **Call** `StartGame`.

You can see that the `StartGame` function is called only when a player breaks a block. This function runs every single time a player breaks a block. Now the player has to step on the blocks.

```
★ function main
  Arena
  do function   function StartGame ▼   when [ block_break ▼ Event ] happens
```

4 Run the mod in Minecraft.

Make sure that when you break the `melon` block, you're put into Survival mode.

5 Set up the respawn function.

A player who dies *respawns* (comes back to life) to the center of the arena.

» Create a new function called `SetupPlayer` (just like you create your `main` function).

» Click the star next to your function and drag an `input name` block into the function.

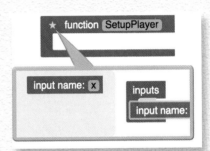

» Change `x` to `info` and click the star again to close the parameter box.

6 Figure out the name of the player that just respawned.

» Make a new variable called `respawn_player`.

» Click the Variables category and drag a `Set item to` block into the `SetupPlayer` function.

» Click the drop-down menu next to the word item and click New Variable. Name it `respawn_player` and click OK.

Your work should now look like what you see in this code.

7 Under the Misc category, drag an item's default block and place it inside the `respawn_player` variable that you just created.

8 **Choose info from the item drop-down menu and replace default with Player.**

To get the player's name, do the same thing you did to get the player, but name the variable `player_name` and get `respawn_player`'s `DisplayName`.

9 **Drag the `do function after` block from the Minecraft/ Events category, a `function` block from the Misc category, and a `number` block from the Math category.**

Change the number to **2000**. Arrange them like you see in this code.

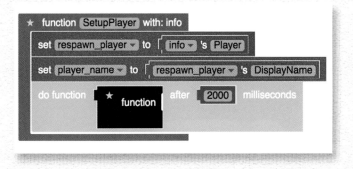

10 **From the Entities category, drag a `Teleport` block into the `function` block and `teleport` me (in the Player category) to `sarah-ArenaBuilder. GetArenaCenter`.**

You'll find it in the Functions category.

11 **Grab a `js` block from the Misc category and type in** on_respawn(player_name)**, like you see on the next page.**

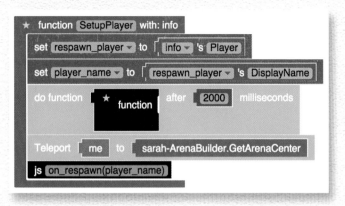

12 Set up the respawn event.

13 Add a `js` block (from the Misc category) to your `main` function and type it just the way it is here:
events.when("player. PlayerRespawnEvent",SetupPlayer,me,false)

14 The `JavaScript` block calls the event `PlayerRespawnEvent`, which requires these parameters:

» The function to call when the player respawns.

» The player who is respawning.

» A `true` or `false` value that tells the mod whether this is a `BedSpawn`. (Use the `false` value because you don't want to teleport back to your bed.)

The `SetupPlayer` function gets data from the info parameter, but this time the `info` parameter is a player, not a block.

Events can be tricky, but if you need help you can always review badges that you've already earned or ask questions on the LearnToMod forums.

15 Run the mod and break the `melon` block.

When you do that, the game mode should switch to Survival.

16 Break a `diamond` block and fall.

Two seconds after you respawn, you're in the arena again.

You have a game! But unless you break a `diamond` block, you never lose. In the next section, I help you find a way to make the game more challenging.

CHALLENGE: MAKE BLOCKS DISAPPEAR ONE SECOND AFTER TOUCHING THEM

To add the first challenge to the game, you need to create another event. This time, when the player moves, a function is called that finds the location of the player. It replaces the block below the player with an `air` block.

1 Add the `removeBlockAfterStep` function.

2 Add the `removeBlock` function.

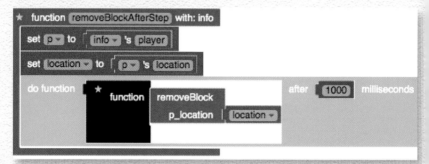

3 Make a call to them from the `main` function.

Now the entire Spleef mod should look like what you see on the next page.

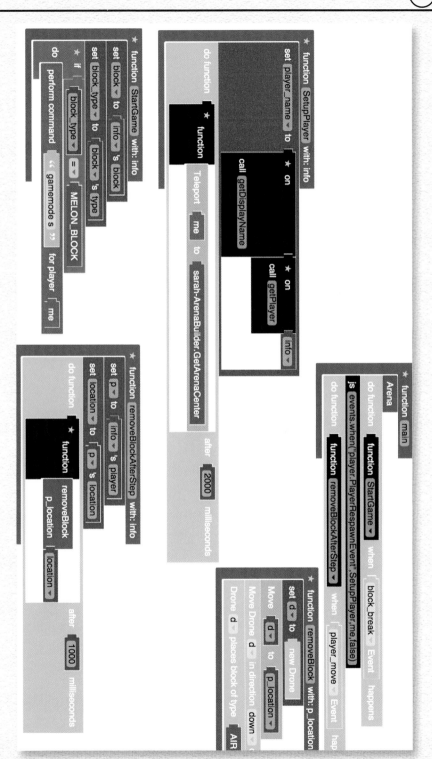

(Code continues from the previous page.)

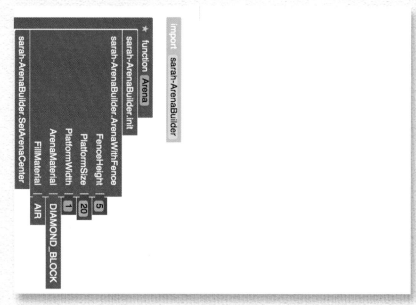

4 Test out the game.

Try these sample test cases for the Spleef mod:

» **The scene sets up correctly:** When you run the mod, two arenas appear: a brick arena with lava and a diamond arena with a tall fence.

» **The player is put into a different mode when the `melon` block breaks:** When you break the `melon` block, the player is set to Survival mode.

» **Blocks disappear:** One second after you touch a block, it disappears.

» **Lava changes player health:** When the player falls into the lava, he loses all his health. (This should be true because the player is in Survival mode, but you should still check that it happens.)

» **Respawn back to arena:** Two seconds after the player respawns, she automatically returns to the arena.

Remember earlier in this project, when you used a *conditional* statement to check if the player broke the `melon` block: If one thing is true, do Step A, and if it isn't true, do Step B? You can add a conditional statement that makes sure you're walking on a `diamond` block before it changes to an `air` block.

You can see the blocks you need to add to the `removeBlock` function to check the type of block you're walking on.

REWARD: GIVE THE PLAYER POINTS

Points can be the number of blocks that the player destroys before falling through the platform. You just have to count the number of blocks that get converted to `air`.

Follow these steps:

1 **Add to the StartGame function a new variable named blocksDestroyed and set it to 0.**

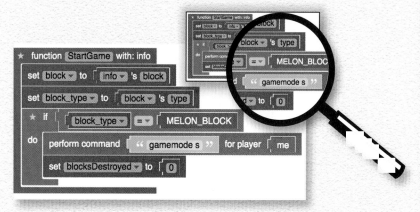

2 **Add 1 to the blocksDestroyed variable.**

You should add **1** to the blocks_destroyed variable every time you place an air block in the removeBlock function. That's how you're destroying blocks — you're replacing them with air.

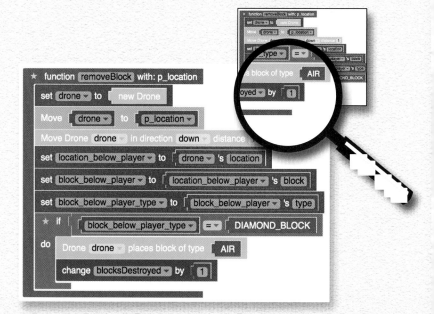

3 Add a Send message **block to the** SetupPlayer **function.**

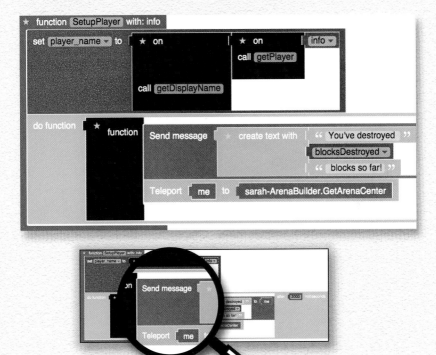

That lets a player know how many blocks she destroyed before falling through the platform.

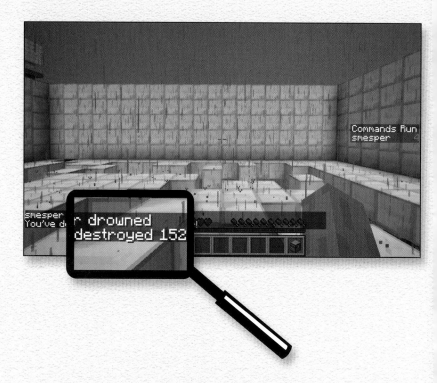

Now when you play the Spleef game, a message appears after you respawn.

You finished an entire iteration of the gameplay loop for your Spleef game. Flex — you showed some real Minecraft muscle.

MAKE SPLEEF: ITERATION 2

After you do one iteration of the Spleef game and play the heck out of it, you might be ready to repeat the gameplay loop and do something more challenging.

In this section, I walk you through four examples in each part of the gameplay loop so that you can

» Add a lava platform underneath the diamond arena.

» Challenge your player to destroy 200 blocks.

» Add an enemy (another challenge for players).

» Add fireworks (a reward).

START: ADD A LAVA PLATFORM

After you have a working game, you can add lava to the scene. Everyone knows what happens when you fall into lava.

Because you're using the ArenaBuilder library, you don't have to make many changes to the Spleef code. You can see here what call to add to the `arena` function. When you add it, you get a different scene.

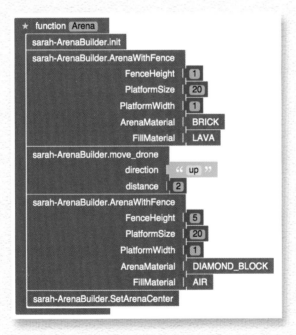

GOAL: DESTROY AT LEAST 200 BLOCKS

Your mod already counts the number of blocks that the player destroys. You can reward your players even more by adding to the `removeBlock` function. Congratulate the player on becoming a Master Spleefer.

CHALLENGE: ADD AN ENEMY

Nobody needs enemies, but they sure do make games more lively. You can add an enemy to the arena by using the `melon` block as the spawning point.

Spawn a creeper in a random spot in the arena. Then the player has to avoid the creeper and try not to fall before destroying 200 blocks.

REWARD: ADD FIREWORKS

You've challenged your players plenty, so make sure they get plenty of rewards. Besides congratulating players, you can give them a fireworks show!

Add the `Fireworks` block to the `removeBlock` function.

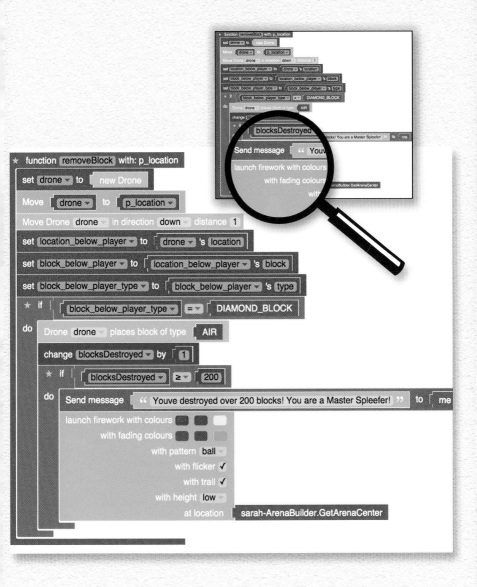

```
★ function removeBlock with: p_location

set drone ▾ to   new Drone

Move   drone ▾  to   p_location ▾

Move Drone drone ▾ in direction down ▾ distance 1

set location_below_player ▾ to   drone ▾ 's location

set block_below_player ▾ to   location_below_player ▾ 's block

set block_below_player_type ▾ to   block_below_player ▾ 's type

★ if   block_below_player_type ▾  = ▾  DIAMOND_BLOCK

do   Drone drone ▾ places block of type   AIR

     change blocksDestroyed ▾ by 1

     ★ if   blocksDestroyed ▾  ≥ ▾  200

     do  Send message  " Youve destroyed over 200 blocks! You are a Master Spleefer! "  to   me

         launch firework with colours  ▪ ▪ ▫
               with fading colours  ▪ ▪ ▫
                    with pattern ball ▾
                    with flicker ✓
                    with trail ✓
                    with height low ▾
                    at location   sarah-ArenaBuilder.GetArenaCenter
```

The Fireworks block is under the World category.

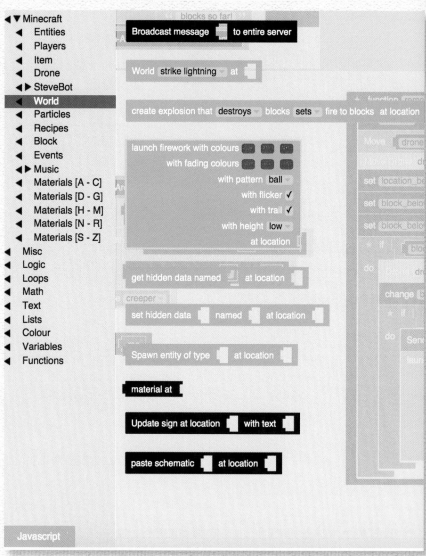

PROJECT **3** *MONSTER ARENA*

MONSTER ARENA IS A MULTILEVEL MINECRAFT MINIGAME WHERE THE PLAYER IS IN A LARGE ARENA WITH MONSTERS THAT SPAWN AROUND A MELON CUBE BLOCK. The player's goal is to reach the melon cube without being attacked by the monsters. Every time the player reaches the melon cube, he moves on to the next level, which has more monsters that are harder to beat.

In this project you make a Monster Arena mod. Then you can play Monster Arena with your friends and see who can defeat the most monsters!

DRAW THE GAMEPLAY LOOP

Draw the gameplay loop (see the next page) for the Monster Arena game. It will work just how it did in the project before this one.

» **Start:** Build the arena.

» **Goal:** Break the `melon` block.

» **Challenge:** Add monsters.

» **Reward:** Level up.

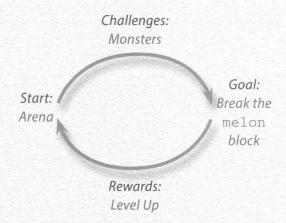

Challenges:
Monsters

Start:
Arena

Goal:
Break the
`melon`
block

Rewards:
Level Up

This project helps you make each iteration of the gameplay loop harder to beat. To start, you have a simple arena with one `melon` block, one monster, and one level.

Iterate *means to do something over and over. Every time you do that something, you make progress. For example, if you iterate on the gameplay loop, you add a feature (like a new challenge or reward).*

ITERATION 1: MAKE MONSTER ARENA

Here's one way to tackle the first iteration of the gameplay loop:

1 **Start: Create a basic arena enclosed by a fence.**

In Monster Arena, the arena is round. A large fence surrounds the arena to keep the player and monsters inside it.

2 **Goal: Add a `melon` block to break.**

For this minigame, you also need to write code to reset the arena when the player breaks the `melon` block.

3 Challenge: Add monsters to the arena.

You add one monster to the arena, and the player has to avoid the monster while trying to break the `melon` block. If the player breaks the `melon` block, the game resets.

Ask your friends to test your game after you add monsters. They'll probably say that it isn't hard to play, but they can tell you what kinds of challenges they like. Do they want more monsters or a bigger arena?

4 Reward: Replay the first level.

In the first iteration, the user who breaks the `melon` block is the one who gets to play Level 1 again. In Iteration 2, you add more levels.

After you plan out the gameplay loop in Steps 1–4, it's time to build Monster Arena.

Whenever you build any game, the first thing you need is a basic scene.

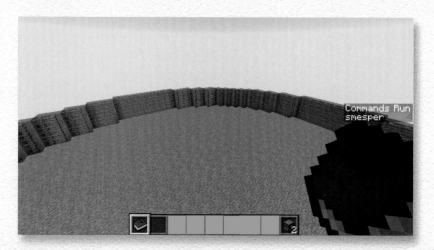

START: CREATE A BASIC ARENA WITH A FENCE

You may already know that the *radius* is the line from the middle of a circle to any point on the circle's edge. Everything in Minecraft is made with blocks.

Just count the blocks between the center and the edge of the circle — that is the arena's radius.

Monster Arena needs this stuff:

» A place for the player and monster to run around

» A way to make sure that the monsters and player can't leave the area

For this basic scene, you create

» A platform

» A fence

In the Spleef project you built an arena using the LearnToMod library named `sarah-ArenaBuilder`. That library makes square arenas. This time you need a round one. Use WorldEdit commands to make the arena in LearnToMod!

A *WorldEdit* command can run in Minecraft to edit the world.

You can explore lots of WorldEdit commands online. Search for the term minecraft worldedit commands *using a search engine. Visit wiki.sk89q.com/wiki/WorldEdit (the official WorldEdit wiki) to see a list of all WorldEdit commands for Minecraft. Just click a link to a category (like Filling Pits, which is under Utilities).*

WorldEdit commands work when you're connected to the LearnToMod Minecraft Server. Follow the instructions on the Minecraft Connect badge if you don't know how to connect to the LearnToMod Minecraft Server.

TEST WORLDEDIT COMMANDS IN MINECRAFT

Before you make the arena, test out the WorldEdit commands in Minecraft.

WIKI WIKI WIKI

A *wiki* is an information website that people can add to and edit. Wikipedia, for example, is a website that has pages on thousands of topics. Each page (like the Minecraft page) is added to and edited by people who know about Minecraft.

Cylinders and circles

- //cyl <block> <radius> [height]
- //hcyl <block> <radius> [height]

WorldEdit is capable of producing both hollow and filled cylinders as well as hollow and filled circles. It uses a fast algorithm to generate the objects and the algorithm is capable of creating nice and symmetrical edges. The cylinders are created at your feet and extend upwards. If you are creating a circle, you simply only need to create a cylinder of height 1.

Example: Creating a filled glass cylinder of radius 5 and height 10
//cyl glass 5 10

Example: Creating a hollow glass circle of radius 5
//hcyl glass 5 1

To make the round arena, you create a *cylinder* (like a tube) and a circle. Those WorldEdits are in the Generation category on the wiki. (It's toward the bottom of the page.)

First you type the code to make

> » a platform
>
> » made of stone
>
> » with a radius of 20

Type this: **//cyl stone 20**. Then you see the platform.

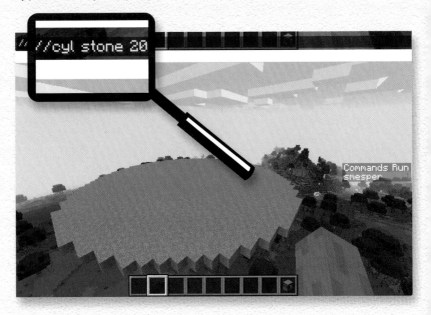

When you're trying to build a large structure, double-click the spacebar to hover, and then click your mouse and hold the spacebar to move up into the sky before running your mod. This action creates the large platform in the sky and makes it easier to see the arena.

Try making the fence with WorldEdit commands. If you don't move, you can make a wooden fence inside the stone fence. Just enter the code that follows the kind of fence:

> » Stone fence: //hcyl stone 20 4
>
> » Wooden fence: //hcyl fence 19 4

If you move after you create the platform and before you create the fence, your fence won't fit perfectly around the platform.

If you call `//cyl stone 20` *and* `//hcyl stone 20 4` *and* `//hcyl fence 19 4` without moving, you wind up with an arena with a fence around it.

Calling code means that Minecraft will handle that task. You don't have to build the cylinder by hand, one block at a time.

MOD THE ARENA IN LEARNTOMOD

After you test the WorldEdit commands, call them from the LearnToMod mod. Crazy idea — I know.

To call WorldEdit commands from LearnToMod, you have to use a `PerformCommand` *block. It's under the Players category.*

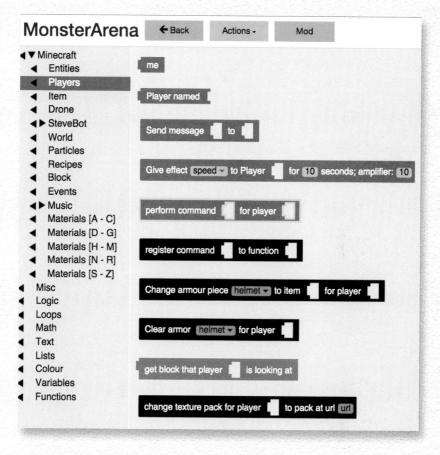

When you use a `PerformCommand` block, the first slash mark (/) is already included, so you need to have only *one* slash mark to make the platform and fences. You can see here what the `main` function looks like for the initial scene.

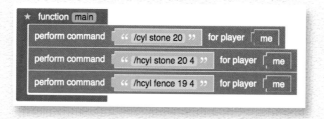

Test your mod to make sure that it's the right kind of arena.

REFACTOR: MOVE THE ARENA CODE TO A NEW FUNCTION

Before you add a goal, refactor your code so that the `main` function stays simple. You can see here how to refactor your code to clean up the `main` function.

Refactoring *code means to change the way it looks without changing what it does. Refactoring is useful for you as a coder because it can make it easier for you to understand the code later on.*

GOAL: ADD A MELON BLOCK TO BREAK

The `arena` function stays the same, but now add a `melon` block on the opposite side of the arena from the player.

Here's the new function, `SetupGame`, which places the `melon` block and puts the player in the starting position. The next steps help you make the `SetupGame` function.

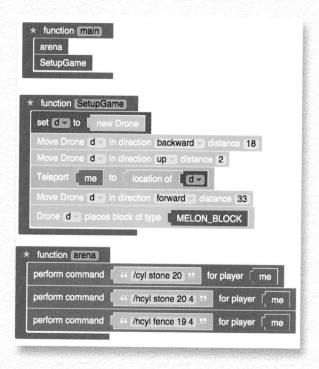

To add a `melon` block, follow these steps:

1 **Create the SetupGame function and add a call to SetupGame to main.**

2 **Add a new drone named d and move it to one side of the arena.**

The drone should move only 18 blocks because the stone and the fence take up 2 blocks, and you want the player *inside* the fence.

3 **Move the drone up by 2.**

This makes the player start above the platform and fall into the arena.

4 **Move the player to the location of the drone.**

Now the player's at the starting spot.

5 **Move the drone 33 blocks to the opposite side of the arena.**

That leaves two blocks empty between the `melon` block and the fence.

6 **Place the `melon` block and move the drone backward by 1 block.**

For right now, nothing happens when the player breaks the `melon` block. You write that code in Iteration 2.

TEST: MAKE SURE YOUR GAME WORKS

Test your mod by dragging it from your mod chest into your HotBar and then clicking to run it. You should see this scene when you run the mod.

CHALLENGE: ADD MONSTERS TO THE ARENA

After your game is all set up, you can start making it playable. On the first iteration of the gameplay loop, add one monster for the player to beat (or to avoid, at least).

This time, write the code to spawn the monster in a separate function from the beginning. This code makes a monster spawn near the `melon` block. The drone is at the `melon` block, so it moves backward (toward the player) and then spawns the creeper.

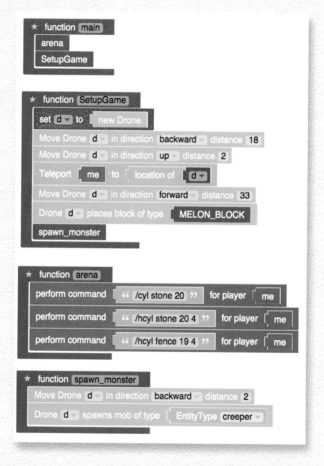

Before you spawn the creeper, move the drone 1 block away from the `melon` block. That way the creeper doesn't spawn inside the block and just die.

Now when you test your game, you see a screen like this. That's one nasty monster!

REWARD: REPLAY THE FIRST LEVEL

In other iterations you reward players with harder levels. (Who'd think of a harder game as a reward?) For this first iteration, however, just let people replay the first level.

First you make a function that gets called when the break block event happens. The on_block_break function checks to see if the melon block was broken. If it was, you see the message "Yay! You broke the Melon Block!"

Follow the steps to make this function:

1 **Create a function and call it on_block_break (like you did to create the SetupGame function).**

2 **Create a variable called event_block and put an info's block inside the variable.**

The event_block is in the Variables category. The info's block is in the Misc category.

3 Make a variable called `event_block_type` and put an `event_block`'s type inside it.

4 From the Logic category, drag an `if` block and an `=` block and compare the `event_block_type` variable to the `MELON_BLOCK` (in the Materials H-M category).

5 Send this message: Yay! You broke the Melon Block!

Next, you'll actually call the `on_block_break` function when the player breaks a block.

6 Click the Minecraft and then Events category and drag a `do function when happens` block and put it in your `main` function.

7 Under the Misc category, grab the `function` block that has a drop-down menu and put it in the first empty spot in the `do function when happens` block.

8 Click the down arrow to change the function to `on_block_break`.

9 Grab an `Event` block from under the Minecraft and then Events category. Change the event to `block_break` by clicking the blue down arrow.

You've made an event that calls the `on_block_break` function whenever the player breaks any block. This code shows how to add this *event call* into the `main` function.

If you don't remember how to do some (or any) of these parts, look at the pictures in this book and go through all the categories until you find the right blocks. You can also post on the forum at *forum.learntomod.com* and ask for help, or go back and earn badges under the Learn tab at *mod.learntomod.com*.

Now you want that person to restart the level.

10 **Add two variables to the** `SetupGame` **function:**

» One keeps track of where the player should start out.

» One puts down the `melon` block.

This code shows how to add these two variables.

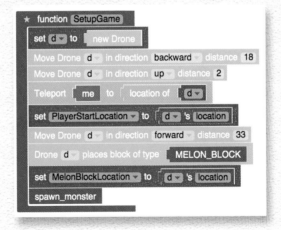

11 Write a `ResetGame` **function that does this stuff:**

» Destroys all monsters in the arena

» Teleports the player back to the starting position

» Moves drone `d` back to the `melon` block's starting spot

» Makes a new `melon` block

» Spawns monsters again

This code shows the new function.

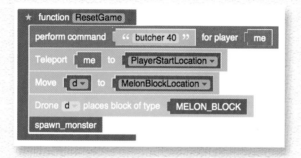

This code shows how to call it from the `on_block_break` function.

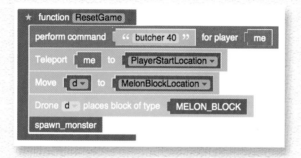

TEST: ITERATION 1 COMPLETED

After you finish the four parts of Iteration 1, you can test your game and make sure that everything works. Your code should look like this.

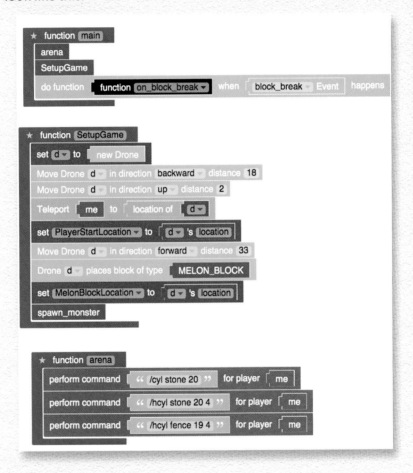

(Code continues on the next page.)

```
★ function on_block_break with: info
    set event_block ▾ to    info ▾ 's block
    set event_block_type ▾ to    event_block ▾ 's type
    ★ if    event_block_type ▾ = ▾    MELON_BLOCK
    do    Send message    " Yay! You broke the Melon Block! "    to    me
          ResetGame
```

```
★ function ResetGame
    perform command    " butcher 40 "    for player    me
    Teleport    me    to    PlayerStartLocation ▾
    Move    d ▾    to    MelonBlockLocation ▾
    Drone    d ▾    places block of type    MELON_BLOCK
    spawn_monster
```

```
★ function spawn_monster
    Move Drone    d ▾    in direction    backward ▾    distance    2
    Drone    d ▾    spawns mob of type    EntityType creeper ▾
```

When you're testing, try a few test cases. That makes sure that you've tested everything you've written. (Project 2 explains testing.)

ITERATION 2: ADD LEVELS

On Iteration 2 of the Monster Arena gameplay loop, you can

» Add more levels.

» Make the arena different.

» Have the player break a different item.

START: MAKE THE ARENA UNIQUE

Add some designs to the arena floor. Take your time. Be creative. Use the platform or the fences. You might even want to add a ceiling to the arena!

I used two `//hcyl` WorldEdit commands to make one hollow *cylinder* (tube) of glass and one of diamond.

You can see the code for changed `arena` function.

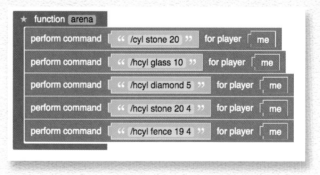

If you add a ceiling, start your player inside the arena. Otherwise, that person will be locked out.

GOAL: WAIT UNTIL A LATER ITERATION

Sometimes when you're going through the gameplay loop, you don't want to change one of the sections — like when your goal is still the same. No problem. You don't have to make any changes to the goal this time around.

Kick back. Relax for a minute.

CHALLENGE: ADD MONSTERS

Moving around one creeper isn't the hardest thing in the world. It's time to add more monsters.

By making one small change to the `spawn_monster` function with the number 5, you can spawn five creepers instead of one. Now your player is outnumbered!

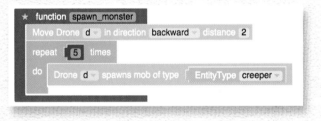

REWARD: ADD A SECOND LEVEL

In Monster Arena, levels are different based on what monsters there are. To add a second level, follow these steps:

1 **Create a variable named** Level. **Start the variable at** 1.

It keeps track of which level the player is on. It starts at 1 because the player starts on the first level.

2 **Make a list of monsters.**

3 **Name the list** Monsters.

4 **Add two types of monsters: creepers and zombies.**

CLEAN YOUR ROOM

Variables are just a way of naming a piece of information, data, or an object. It's kind of like how my name is Sarah and when my mom wants me to do something she says, "Sarah, clean your room." That lets me know that I have to be the one to clean my room.

Computers work the same way! You, as a coder, will name information. When you want the computer to use that information, use its name. For example, you made a variable that keeps track of the type of block that's broken. That way you can ask the computer to test whether it was the same type as a MELON_BLOCK.

This code shows how to create these two variables in the SetupGame function.

```
★ function SetupGame
  set d ▼ to    new Drone
  Move Drone d ▼ in direction backward ▼ distance 18
  Move Drone d ▼ in direction up ▼ distance 2
  Teleport   me  to  location of   d ▼
  set PlayerStartLocation ▼ to   d ▼ 's location
  Move Drone d ▼ in direction forward ▼ distance 33
  Drone d ▼ places block of type    MELON_BLOCK
  set MelonBlockLocation ▼ to   d ▼ 's location
  set Level ▼ to  1
  set Monsters ▼ to   ★ create list with  EntityType creeper ▼
                                           EntityType zombie ▼
  spawn_monster
```

5 **Change the** `spawn_monster` **function to spawn a different monster depending on what level you're on.**

If you change your code in your `spawn_monster` function to look just like the following code, the monsters change based on the level.

The code you change chooses the correct item from the list.

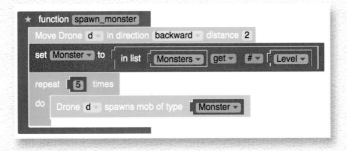

6 **Increase the level variable every time the player breaks the** `melon` **block.**

7 **If the player reaches the final level (right now that's Level 2), tell her that the game is finished. If she hasn't reached the last level yet, this game should reset with the new monsters.**

The code on the next page shows what changes you have to make in `on_block_break` that need to happen to start the new level.

```
★  function  on_block_break  with: info
   set  event_block ▼  to    info ▼  's  block
   set  event_block_type ▼  to    event_block ▼  's  type
   ★  if      event_block_type ▼    = ▼    MELON_BLOCK
   do   Send message    " Yay! You broke the Melon Block! "  to   me
        change  Level ▼  by   1
        ★  if      Level ▼    > ▼    2
        do   Send message    " Yay! You beat all of the levels! Good job! "  to   me
        else   ResetGame
```

TEST: MAKE SURE BOTH LEVELS WORK

After you add the changes to the spawn_monster function, test your mod. When you start the test, you should see five creepers.

If you break the melon block, the game resets and you see five zombies.

If you break the melon block again, you see the message "Yay! You beat all of the levels! Good job!"

ITERATION 3: ADD LEVELS TO YOUR LEVELS

After you start getting the hang of making the Monster Arena minigame, you can feel good adding a few more levels and challenges.

You can skip the Start and Goal sections in Iteration 3. The game is becoming fun because you're adding more challenges and rewards.

CHALLENGE: SWITCH TO SURVIVAL MODE

You may have noticed that it's pretty easy for a player to get past all the creatures. That's because the player is in Creative mode.

1 Add a `perform command` block.

The code shows the changes you make to the `SetupGame` function to do this. You only change the last block of the function — just add the `perform command` block.

When the game starts, the player goes into Survival mode.

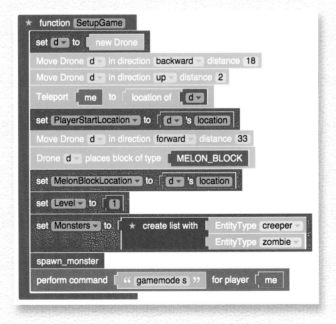

Now that you've made it easier for the player to die, you should include an event that happens when the player respawns.

2 **Change the** `main` **function and create the new** `RespawnPlayer` **function.**

Look at code in the book and compare it to your code. You should be able to figure out what's missing in your code and how to add it. But don't worry! If you ever get stuck, just go to forum.learntomod.com and ask for help!

3 **In the** `main` **function, add a** `js` **block (found in the Misc category) that has this code in it:** `events. when("player.PlayerRespawnEvent", RespawnPlayer,me,false)`.

4 **Create a new function called** `RespawnPlayer`. **It should look exactly like this code.**

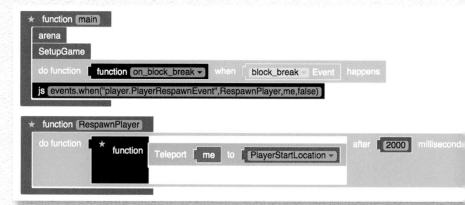

I'll let you figure out how to make it by looking at the correct code here in the book. Create it from scratch. I know you can do it! After you have made the new `RespawnPlayer` function and made the changes to the `main` function, the player teleports back to the arena when she respawns.

REWARD: ADD FIVE MORE LEVELS

Adding levels is pretty easy because you already set up the levels to be based on a list. To make more levels, follow these steps:

1 **Change the conditional statement so it's based on the list length.**

To refactor means to change the way code looks without changing what it does.

You're making sure that you iterated through all the monsters in the Monster List (instead of a specific number, like 2).

The code shows how to change the conditional statement to have it based on the list length. Figure out the one place you should change your code. (Hint: You aren't checking if Level is less than 2. You're checking if Level is less than the length of a list.)

```
★ function on_block_break with: info
  set event_block ▼ to    info ▼ 's block
  set event_block_type ▼ to    event_block ▼ 's type
  ★ if     event_block_type ▼  = ▼    MELON_BLOCK
  do  Send message  " Yay! You broke the Melon Block! "  to   me
      change Level ▼ by  1
      ★ if    Level ▼  > ▼    length of   Monsters ▼
      do  Send message  " Yay! You beat all of the levels! Good job! "  to   me
      else  ResetGame
```

A conditional statement is one that compares two things. You can read it like a sentence. For example, if level is greater than the length of monsters, then send a message; otherwise, reset the game.

2 **Change the `SetupGame` function to add monsters to your Monster List.**

The code shows the updated `SetupGame` function. Add entities to the Monster List. You can find them under Minecraft and then Entities. Change which one you're adding by clicking the yellow arrow and choosing from the list.

To add more positions into a list, click the star on next to the words `create list with` *and drag* `item` *blocks into the list block.*

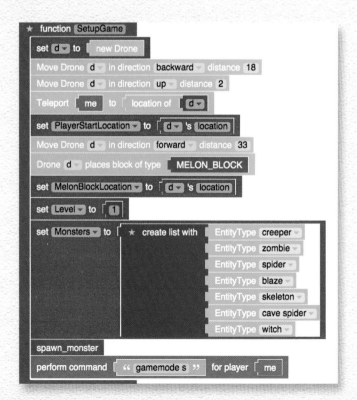

3 **Change the** `spawn_monster` **function.**

This code shows how to spawn more monsters as the levels get harder.

```
★ function spawn_monster
    Move Drone  d  in direction  backward  distance  2
    set  Monster ▾  to      in list  Monsters ▾   get ▾   # ▾   Level ▾
    repeat     5   x ▾   Level ▾     times
    do     Drone  d ▾  spawns mob of type    Monster ▾
```

MAKE MORE ITERATIONS: BE CREATIVE AND UNIQUE

If you followed the steps in this project, you created an entire multilevel Monster Arena minigame! (Yay! You made so many levels! Good job!)

Keep iterating on the gameplay loop to make *more* challenges, *new* rewards, and *different* goals. You can change the arena by adding patterns to the platform.

 A more challenging addition is to add random monsters at each level.

For example, at Level 1 you add five creepers, and at Level 2 you add ten monsters that are (randomly) creepers or zombies. At Level 3, you add a total of 15 monsters that are (randomly) creepers, zombies, or spiders.

This code shows how to add randomness to the `spawn_monster` function.

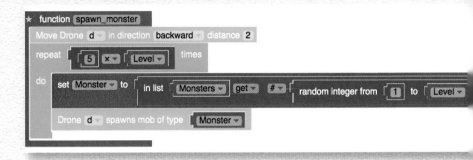

PROJECT 4 CAPTURE THE FLAG

HAVE YOU EVER PLAYED CAPTURE THE FLAG? You play like this: Each player gets at least one flag (actually a glowstone block). Each player hides her flag in the world, and if the player dies (maybe because she fell into some lava), she could respawn anywhere there's a flag. The trick is to make sure you hide your flags well. If you run out of flags, you won't be able to respawn anywhere.

In this project you're going to make a basic Capture the Flag game, play it with a friend, then add magic wands to make the game even more fun. Everyone needs a bit more magic, right?

USE THE CAPTURE THE FLAG LIBRARY

To set up your game using the Capture the Flag library, follow these steps:

1 Create a new mod called `Magical_Capture_The_Flag`.

2 Go to the code page.

You should see a blank mod.

3 Go into the Misc category and drag the `import` block into the coding area.

Now you've imported my Capture the Flag mod.

 You have to spell and capitalize my Capture the Flag library exactly like you see it here. Otherwise, it won't work.

4 Import `sarah-CaptureTheFlag`.

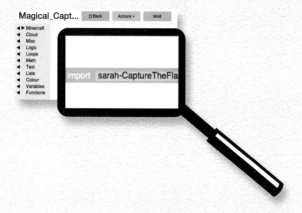

You should see some new functions under the Functions category. You can start making your Capture the Flag mod!

MAKE A BASIC CAPTURE THE FLAG

You're going to play your game with a friend. These steps help you set up your main function so that you and one other person can play together:

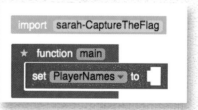

1 **Create a new variable called PlayerNames.**

2 **Drag the create list with block out of the List category.**

   It has three positions, but you only need two.

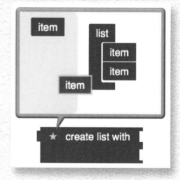

3 **Click the star and drag one of the item blocks out of the list.**

4 **Click the star again to close it.**

TRY IT OUTSIDE, TOO

Capture the Flag is an old game based on war. You see, flags show that a place is your territory, your area. For a long time since, kids played the game outside with pieces of fabric as flags. In the early 1980s, Scholastic released a Capture the Flag–style game on one of the first home computers. Since then, lots of makers have used it to make their own games (like Halo and Team Fortress 2).

5 In the list, type your Minecraft username and your friend's Minecraft username.

 You have to spell and capitalize usernames exactly right. Otherwise, they won't work.

6 Bring the `sarah-CaptureTheFlag.init` function into your `main` function.

7 Use a `for each item in list` block from the Loop category.

8 Rename `i` as `PlayerName`.

9 Add the `PlayerName` variable to the end of the block.

10 Add a call to the `sarah-CaptureTheFlag.give_flag` function from the Functions category.

11 Pass `glowstone`, `PlayerName`, and `1` in as parameters.

12 Add a `perform command` block from the Players category.

The game mode changes to Survival for each player.

13 Add the entire loop to your `main` function.

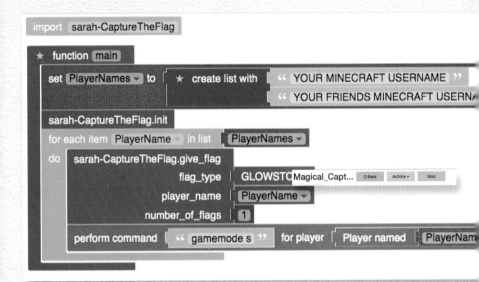

```
import  sarah-CaptureTheFlag

★ function main
    set PlayerNames ▾ to   ★ create list with   " YOUR MINECRAFT USERNAME "
                                                 " YOUR FRIENDS MINECRAFT USERN/

    sarah-CaptureTheFlag.init
    for each item PlayerName ▾ in list   PlayerNames ▾
    do    sarah-CaptureTheFlag.give_flag
                        flag_type    GLOWSTO Magical_Capt...  □ Back   Actions ▾   Mod
                        player_name    PlayerName ▾
                        number_of_flags    1
              perform command  " gamemode s "  for player   Player named   PlayerNam
```

You have a two-player game. Grab a friend or your grandma and try the next section.

TEST YOUR TWO-PLAYER CAPTURE THE FLAG

Now it's time to test your game. Follow these steps:

1 Click the Mod button at the top of your mod.

2 Join your LearnToMod server by opening Minecraft, clicking Multiplayer, and clicking the LearnToMod server.

It's the server that you created in the first project.

3 **Type** /open.

```
You have opened your server.
Tell your friends to join play.learntomod.com
And run the command /join 227

/open_
```

4 **Have your friend join his LearnToMod server on his own computer and type in** /join ##.

Your friend has to have his own LearnToMod account for this to work, so make sure he is signed up at mod.learntomod.com.

Instead of typing ##, your friend should type the number that appeared in your server. For example, if you were joining my server, you'd type /join 227.

5 **Run your mod.**

You and your friend should each get one glowstone block in your HotBar. You should both be in Survival mode. You can tell because you'll see hearts above your HotBar.

6 **Put your glowstone block somewhere.**

When you die and respawn, you wind up at your glowstone block after two seconds. If this doesn't work, head to forum.learntomod.com and see if anyone there has run into the same problem. You can also carefully go through each block that you made and the pictures in this book to see what's different between the two. Multiplayer games are tricky! It's smart to ask for help if you're having trouble.

ADD WANDS

Wands can make your game more interesting. Follow these steps to add some:

1 **Drag the** `import` **block into your mod.**

2 **Type** sarah-magic_wands **in the space.**

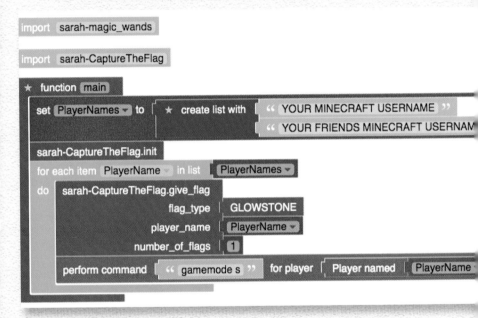

When you open the Functions category, you'll see a lot of functions about magic wands.

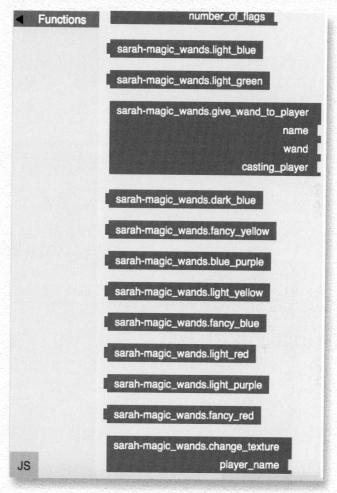

5 Add a call to the `sarah-magic_wands.give_wand_to_player` **function into your** `main` **function.**

You can find the function in the Functions category now that you've imported my `magic_wands` library.

4 **Pass in these as parameters:**

» `ExplosionWand`

» `sarah-magic_wands.light-green` (in the Functions category)

» `Player` named `PlayerName`

5 **Test your game again.**

You and your friend should get a wand (which looks like a disc) and a flag.

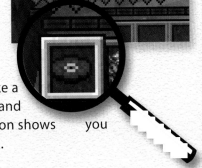

Well that's cool! A wand shaped like a bagel. The only thing is that the wand *doesn't do anything*. The next section shows you how to attach magic to your wand.

ATTACH MAGIC TO YOUR WANDS

What's a wand without magic? A bagel, that's what.

It's time to make your Capture the Flag a magical game:

1 **Import the** `sarah-Exploding_Projectile` **library.**

2 **Grab a** `js` **block from the Misc category.**

3 **Type in** events.when("player.PlayerInteractEvent",CastSpells, player, false**.**

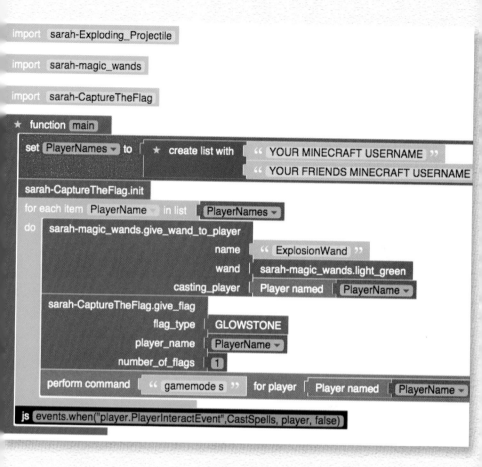

```
import  sarah-Exploding_Projectile

import  sarah-magic_wands

import  sarah-CaptureTheFlag

★ function main

  set PlayerNames ▾ to    ★ create list with    " YOUR MINECRAFT USERNAME "
                                                  " YOUR FRIENDS MINECRAFT USERNAME "
  sarah-CaptureTheFlag.init
  for each item PlayerName ▾ in list  PlayerNames ▾
  do    sarah-magic_wands.give_wand_to_player
                               name        " ExplosionWand "
                               wand        sarah-magic_wands.light_green
                      casting_player       Player named  PlayerName ▾
        sarah-CaptureTheFlag.give_flag
                       flag_type    GLOWSTONE
                     player_name    PlayerName ▾
                 number_of_flags    1
        perform command  " gamemode s "  for player   Player named  PlayerName ▾
  js  events.when("player.PlayerInteractEvent",CastSpells, player, false)
```

You're setting up an event to call a function called
CastSpells. It's called when a player interacts with any
item.

*Make sure to spell and capitalize everything in
the js block exactly the way it's shown in Step 3.
Otherwise, it won't work.*

4 **Create a function called CastSpells. It should take in
one parameter called info.**

To add a parameter, just click the star on the function *block and drag an* input name *block into the function.*

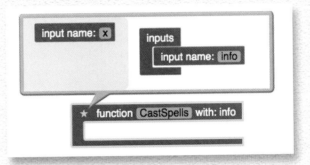

5 **Create two local variables:**

» WandPlayer

» Wand

The local variables are under the Misc category.

6 **From the Misc category, drag the** item's default **block to the** CastSpells **function.**

7 **Change the block to** info Player **and put it in the** WandPlayer **variable.**

8 **Choose the Minecraft category, and then choose the Item category.**

9 **Drag the** `Get item in hand name for player` **block and put it in the** `Wand` **variable.**

`WandPlayer` is the player you're checking.

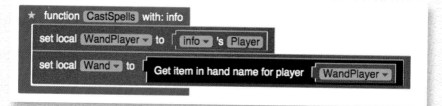

10 **Grab an** `if` **block from the Logic category.**

11 **If the name of the wand is** `ExplosionWand`, **call the** `sarah-Exploding_Projectile.launch` **function.**

`WandPlayer` is the player who's casting the spell or using the wand. Right now, you only know how to call an `ExplosionWand`. If the player interacted with something besides `ExplosionWand`, then it isn't a wand and nothing should happen. You don't want an exploding project every time your player uses a pickaxe.

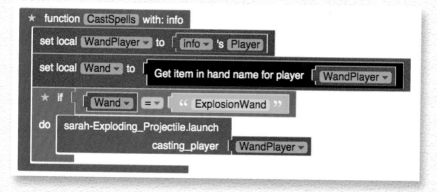

You have magic! In your game, anyway. The code on the next page shows what your code should look like.

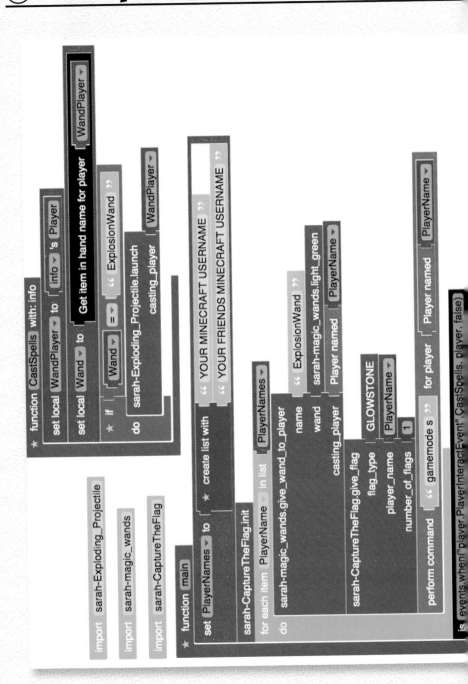

WANDYIER WANDS

 There's a trick you can use to make your wands look more like wands.

Add a call to the `sarah-magic_wands.change_texture` function to your `main` function.

```
★ function main
  set PlayerNames ▾ to    ★ create list with    " YOUR MINECRAFT USERNAME "
                                                 " YOUR FRIENDS MINECRAFT USERNAME "
  sarah-CaptureTheFlag.init
  for each item PlayerName ▾ in list    PlayerNames ▾
  do      sarah-magic_wands.give_wand_to_player
                                    name      " ExplosionWand "
                                    wand      sarah-magic_wands.light_green
                            casting_player    Player named    PlayerName ▾
          sarah-magic_wands.change_texture
                            player_name       PlayerName ▾
          sarah-CaptureTheFlag.give_flag
                            flag_type         GLOWSTONE
                            player_name       PlayerName ▾
                            number_of_flags   1
          perform command    " gamemode s "    for player    Player named    PlayerName ▾
  js  events.when("player.PlayerInteractEvent",CastSpells, player, false)
```

12 Test it.

When you interact with the discwand (or wanddisc or wisc or dand, whichever you like), you should launch a block that explodes when it lands.

MAKE YOUR OWN WAND

You can make your own wand. You could, for example, make one that teleports you to where the `projectile` block lands.

1 Go to mod.learntomod.com/programs/sarah-Exploding_
Projectile.

You should see all of the Exploding_Projectile code.

2 **Click Copy This Mod at the bottom of the modding page.**

When you do, it should say `Successfully Copied!`

3 **Go back to mod.learntomod.com and click the Mod tab.**

4 **Click the `sarah_Exploding_Projectile_ copy` mod tile, and then click Code.**

5 **Click Actions, then Rename.**

6 **Rename the mod `Teleporting_ Projectile` and go to the code for it.**

It should look just like the Exploding_Projectile code does right now.

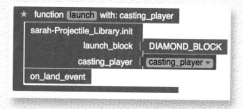

7 **Find the `launch` function. Change the `launch` block to something other than `BEDROCK`.**

You could rename it `DIAMOND_BLOCK`.

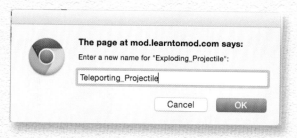

8 **Find the `on_land` function and change the message to say Now Teleporting!**

9 **In the `on_land` function, delete the block that causes the explosion.**

10 Put a `Teleport` **block in the** `Teleport Me to location of info's` **block.**

The `Teleport` block is in the Entities category. Now you have a second wand.

The `Teleport` *and* `location of` *blocks are in the Minecraft, then Entities category. The* Me *block is in the Minecraft, then Players category. The* info's *block is in the Misc category, but you have to change it from* item's *default to* info's *block.*

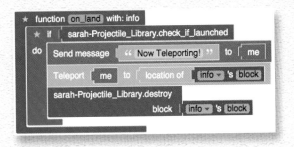

```
import  sarah-Projectile_Library

export  launch

★ function  launch  with: casting_player
    sarah-Projectile_Library.init
              launch_block  |  DIAMOND_BLOCK
            casting_player  |  casting_player ▾
    on_land_event


    ★ function  on_land_event
      set local  event ▾  to  "  entity.EntityChangeBlockEvent  "
      do function    function  on_land ▾    when   event ▾   happens


★ function  on_land  with: info
    ★ if  |  sarah-Projectile_Library.check_if_launched
    do   Send message  "  Now Teleporting!  "  to   me
         Teleport   me   to   location of   info ▾ 's block
         sarah-Projectile_Library.destroy
                    block  |  info ▾ 's block
```

GIVE EACH PLAYER TWO WANDS

When you have the exploding wand and the teleporting wand,
you can go back to your magical Capture the Flag mod and hand
out wands like there's no tomorrow: Give yourself and your friend
one exploding wand and one teleporting wand. Two wands each.
Four wands total. One whole bunch of magic.

1 Import the `sarah-Teleporting_Projectile` mod.

```
import  sarah-Teleporting_Projectile
```

Replace sarah *with your LearnToMod username so you can use your Teleporting_Projectile mod.*

2 Find the CastSpells **function. Click the star on the** if **block. Then drag an** else if **block into the** if **block.**

3 From the Logic category, grab an = **block and put it in the** else if **part of the** if **block.**

4 Put the Wand **variable in the first empty slot. Put a** Text **block that says** TeleportingWand **in the second empty slot.**

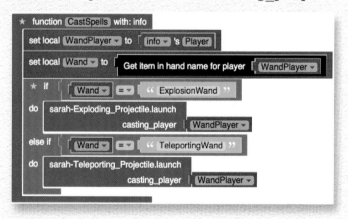

5 From the Functions category, grab a Teleporting_ Projectile.launch **block and put it in the** else if **block.**

The WandPlayer variable is the casting_player.

6 Find the main **function and add a** sarah-magic_ wands.give_wand_to_player **block in the** for each item **loop.**

7 Make sure the three parameters are:

» A Text block with TeleportingWand

» sarah-magic_wands.dark_blue (from the Functions category)

» `Player named` from the Minecraft/Player category and `PlayerName` from the Variables category

Your entire magical Capture the Flag mod should look like this.

(Code continues on the next page.)

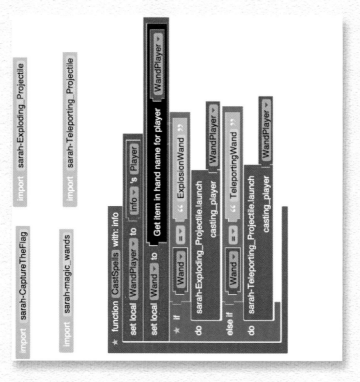

8 Test it out!

When you run it in Minecraft, both you and your friend will each get two wands! The green one causes an explosion and the blue one teleports you, so you can move quickly.

DEDICATION

We dedicate this book to our close friends, and to our families, who have supported us not only in writing this book but also in becoming who we are today. We specifically dedicate this book to Adrian Guthals, who stayed up late at night to battle Sarah in Spleef, Monster Arena, and Capture the Flag. Those games wouldn't have been much fun if Adrian hadn't been there to play-test them.

ABOUT THE AUTHORS

Sarah Guthals, Ph.D., is a computer scientist and an educator who has worked as a programmer at Microsoft, NASA-JPL, and ViaSat. She has also taught hundreds of teachers from around the world how to teach computer science to students as young as 7. Sarah is now the chief technical officer (CTO) and cofounder of ThoughtSTEM, where she develops curriculum and training for teaching computer science through Minecraft modding.

Stephen Foster, Ph.D., is an educator and software engineer who has been developing educational software for teaching coding throughout his career. Stephen is the CEO of ThoughtSTEM and acts as Lead Developer for ThoughtSTEM's educational technologies, which include LearnToMod and CodeSpells. Stephen paved the way for teaching kids coding through modding Minecraft.

Lindsey Handley, Ph.D., is a scientist and educator with a passion for high quality STEM education for K-12 students. Lindsey is currently the COO of ThoughtSTEM and manages its coding after-school programs and camps in over 25 locations across San Diego. Lindsey also provides support to teachers across the world who want to teach coding in their classrooms using the LearnToMod software.

AUTHORS' ACKNOWLEDGMENTS

We would like to acknowledge all of the hard work that went into making Minecraft, an incredibly fun and open-ended game played by millions around the world. We also want to thank the hard-working coders who helped with LearnToMod — using their fast and creative problem-solving skills, we can help teach kids how to make even more with Minecraft. And, of course, we want to thank the millions of kids around the world who play Minecraft. *You* inspired us to teach coding through Minecraft!

PUBLISHER'S ACKNOWLEDGMENTS

Senior Acquisitions Editor:
Amy Fandrei

Development Editor:
Tonya Maddox Cupp

Special Help: Christine Corry,
Connor Morris

Project Layout: Galen Gruman

Creative Director: Paul Dinovo

Marketing: Melisa Duffy,
Lauren Noens, Raichelle Weller

Launch Consultants: John Helmus,
John Scott